Heartspeak

Dedicated to

Blessed John Paul II

‘Give, and it will be given to you; good measure, pressed down, shaken together, running over, will be put into your lap. For the measure you give will be the measure you get back.’

(Luke 6: 38)

Heartspeak

A Contemplative Chorus

Featuring Poets:

Tom BENTALL
Monika CHMELOVA
Catherine CRUZ, FMVD
Helen DE BORCHGRAVE
Sarah DE NORDWALL
Martin EARLE
Jonathan FORDHAM
Sarah FORDHAM
Kate GOLDING
Justin HARMER
Michael HOARE
Jacqui HOULIHAN
Jean HUBERT
Paula JORDAO, FMVD
Kaye LEE
Gabriel OLEARNIK
Karolina STOLARSKA
Piotr STOLARSKI
Andrew THORNTON-NORRIS
Anna VEREY
Fr Dominic WHITE, OP

Edited by Piotr Stolarski

2012

tignarius

Heartspeak: A Contemplative Chorus edited by Piotr Stolarski, 2nd edition, published in Great Britain by Tignarius Publications, London, 2012

ISBN: 978-1-4716-2131-4

Cover design by Claire Louise Barrie & Leo Earle 2011.
You can visit Claire's graphic and web design portfolio at www.hereismydesign.com.

The cover of this book features elements of Giovanni di Paolo's tempera painting 'Paradise' (c. 1445, The Metropolitan Museum of Art, New York) and a photograph by William Warbey of Pierre Vivant's sculpture 'Traffic Light Tree' in the London Docklands. The photograph by William Warbey is available under a Creative Commons license. By making his photo available for public use, it does not mean that William Warbey endorses this book or the book's use of his photo in any way. William Warbey's Flikr page can be viewed at www.flikr.com/wwarbey.

Printed in Great Britain by www.Lulu.com

For further information please contact Piotr Stolarski at tignarius@yahoo.co.uk

See also: www.tignarius.blogspot.com and www.mcstollie.blogspot.com

Contents

IV: The Place Within..........99

Foreword

They were everywhere, all over Rome: huge posters showing the Risen Jesus, rays of red and white light pouring from his heart. In front, knelt the recently deceased Pope, his head in his hands. Beneath ran the words '*Grazie a voi, Santo Padre*' (Thank you Holy Father).

It was 2005, early April. On the eve of the feast of the Divine Mercy (the image of Christ in the poster), on April 2nd that year John Paul II, the first non-Italian to become Pope in 455 years, had died bringing to an end an extraordinary papacy, that had re-set forever the template of what it meant to be Pope in a secular universe.

When in 1978, Karol Wojtyła, 58 and then Archbishop of Kraków had been elected Pontiff, the Divine Mercy, a series of visions witnessed in the 1930s by the nun Sister Faustyna Kowalska, had been virtually unknown outside Poland. By 2005, she had been declared a saint and the image she had seen of Christ – completed with the words 'Jesus I trust in You' under the feet of the picture – was replicated throughout Catholic parishes across the globe.

For a younger generation, evangelised by the upbeat, joyous faith of John Paul II, who had canonised Kowalska, this image and its accompanying message – that God's mercy was infinite and unquenchable - was shorthand for the Pope's constant theme, that God thirsts to meet man (and woman) in a transforming encounter, heart-to-heart.

What happens next, a spiritual voyage of divine discovery, is a chronicle long told by Christian mystics (such as John Paul II's favoured poet John of the Cross), and it is re-told here in these pages, how when modern men and women in all their dilemma and predicament, allow God to touch pain, and their personal Cross, He transforms their inner universe. Where there was dark, God brings light, where sorrow, joy, where pain, healing, a profound peace.

The poet's gift to give form, colour, shape to an intuited God, present – through Scripture and Sacrament – but unseen empirically was something Pope John Paul II was, as a poet himself, keenly attuned to.

The Artist, he explained, in his 1999 Letter to Artists, possesses a share of God's own creativity. It begins with this quote from the Book of Genesis: 'God saw all that He had made, and it was very good' (Genesis 1, 31). 'The opening page of the Bible presents God as a kind of exemplar of everyone who produces a work' claimed the Pope. 'The human craftsman mirrors the image of God as creator.' Art, he wrote in an echo of Augustine, could point to the Divine origin of all beauty.

His vision honoured Sacred Art, the painting, and sculpture which for centuries had illustrated the Gospels and Old Testament stories.

But Christian Art, Wojtyła argued, had a deeper purpose than mere representation: it could explore modern questions – how to recover from a broken heart? Is there a purpose to living? The answer, Wojtyła suggested was God, the creator, longing to enter the life of his creation.

Ceaselessly, throughout his 27-year papacy, John Paul II pressed home this truth that God desired to enter every aspect of human life – including politics, sex, the economy, – and, with the willing co-operation of man, transform it into His image. Karol Wojtyła's first homily as Pope (October 22, 1978) suggested the scale of this vision: 'Do not be afraid!' he urged. 'Open wide the doors for Christ. To his saving power open the boundaries of states, economic and political systems, the vast fields of culture, development, civilisation.' This was the message he would between 1978 and 2005 bring through his tireless pilgrimages (more than 100 in total) to every inhabited continent in the world, to an audience of millions. Some saw him on television, others in the flesh – an unforgettable experience – 'You felt' as one young Franciscan put it, 'as though in a crowd of thousands, he was speaking to you personally.'

And the God he preached was personal, not abstract, or up there in a heaven far distant from everyday problems. Neither was He a judge, harsh and punishing, burdening the believer with stringent, impossible rules. The God Wojtyła preached was rather the source of all beauty, joy, and blessing, who desired man to follow his law – as expressed through the Apostolic Tradition – out of love, rather than resentful obedience or obligation. ('The Church,' John Paul II wrote 'proposes, she imposes nothing.')

And that is the God you will encounter in these enchanting poems, that sing of finding God's presence in joy, in daily minutiae, but also in the dark places. The accent in each is different in each, but the voice one: each poem weaves a narrative of God's encounter with man and woman, today, yesterday, throughout all the ages.

Bess Twiston Davies

Introduction

Do you speak from the heart? Do you wish others would? Or is that just a (tired) dream in a tough world, where wearing your heart on your sleeve, let alone in your mouth, is courting disaster? Each of us has our values, our principles – and our search. We wrestle together with common dilemmas, yet wrestle as much with each other – ideas and dreams which confront as much as unite. We can experience confusion as well as elation – one minute everything seems to be going for us, the next, we are tempted to despair. The heroes have always been the isolated pioneers in a desert of distrust, indifference, or emptiness; 'bearing their crosses' and not always successfully.

The poets represented in this volume speak from their hearts. Everything from the first paragraph is as true of them as of anyone. What they have in common across the widest variety of styles and interests is that they are Christians. Their inspiration – beyond culture or fashion – is Jesus Christ – their hearts' peak. Hence the title of this anthology of contemporary poems moved by or reflecting the Christian faith. In bringing together as many Christian poets as I could, my intention has been threefold: to testify to God's presence in our lives, provide an open forum for people of various backgrounds and denominations to share insights of faith, and mark the beatification of Pope John Paul II – a great poet-mystic, philosopher, playwright, and modern Christian.

Like John Paul, our act of faith is to be open to life, and therefore our poetry also explores dark places. Our experience of living in a world often 'closed' to God undoubtedly dovetails with those of many non-Christian artists - seeking truth in analogous ways. Thus art in general and poetry in particular become channels for the dialogue of the whole person with God, neighbour, and self, at least implicitly. Three in one, the Trinity of God who is Father, Son and Holy Spirit. This reflection points to the wider importance of poetry and creativity as culture-forming activities: practices integrating all that is good through a mixed vision: of faith and reason, simultaneously active and contemplative. Articulated and facilitated by the Holy Spirit, authentic engagement with life becomes a reciprocal mission of testimony and discovery, a multi-relational journey of listening, preaching, assimilating, and evangelising the modern world.

We may be witnessing in this way already, even joyfully, but don't we need to *cooperate* more as Christians? Evangelisation of (or through) culture also includes 'internal' acculturation, prompting the question: how can these poems serve an 'ecumenical' purpose over and above their value as literary witness to Christ?

The answer is related to the power of the Word and the power of words. God Himself inspires poets to write – they feel a need and compulsion to express truths. Ecumenism will fail if it becomes a cliché or 'dead-letter' platitude, preventing the Holy Spirit from working through Christians' daily lives and experiences. The path to greater unity proceeds providentially, at the formal 'credal' level, but also *indirectly* through forthright, ad hoc, dialogue centred on common prayer- and Bible-study groups, charity work, artistic and musical cooperation (as in Sarah de Nordwall's *Bardschool* movement) and other inter-church endeavours. Many Christians, it seems, yearn to complement an understanding of their own faith by discovering or re-discovering the depths of other traditions in creative contexts, while acknowledging differences and embracing mutual interests and fundamental core truths. Poetry is one vital means of personal expression and growth – a way to explore faith (and enact connections) in a personalistic spirit, with and for others, before God. Just such a personalism and faith of the heart was manifested by mystics throughout the ages, Catholic, Protestant, and Orthodox; and so beautifully by Karol Wojtyła.

In short, poetry can be 'ecumenical' if it is appropriated and used ecumenically, and if the authentic inspirations which prompt it are heeded: 'Speak, Lord, your servant is listening'. Only by *heartspeak* – at times including bold and painful discourse – can former enemies become true friends. For real ecumenism proceeds by a willingness to be changed in Christ and to confront sin and division with love and enthusiasm.

Thus, by beginning with prayer and personal witness, and sharing insights, Christians can build up the 'Church of the gaps' (on the interzone between established denominational allegiances, as exemplified by cross-confessional endeavours) – by co-operating with grace to recognise common faith, *and* common wounds: in a dialectic of mutual love, service, and repentance. One could say that the poems collected here reflect contemporary Christian faith, and echo a new approach towards unity which is being wrought from the ground upwards. Through a non-binding form of expression, solicited but freely shared, a kind of 'scripture' of the heart - which can be read and enjoyed by all - becomes another vehicle for the Spirit. Where 'theology' remains problematic, 'culture' (including theology) steps in to manifest charity and facilitate exploration of truth while respecting boundaries of conscience. (Finally, these two mutual accommodations: of Christians with non-Christians, and between Christians, may be synthesised; further relating to one another in trinitarian synergy – a heartfelt chorus – building up the City of God on earth in cooperative self-gift.)

If these poems challenge us, perplex us, or please us – they have moved something within us: something worth exploring. In this way, we allow God to make use of the deep yearnings of our hearts, and grow closer – authentically and joyfully.

Piotr Stolarski, May 2011

Karol Wojtyła: Art and Contemplation

I first came across the poetry of Karol Wojtyła as a teenager. I found a copy of his collection *Easter Vigil* in a charity shop. My then tentative interest in poetry, and faltering spiritual search, must have propelled me to open this most unappealing looking volume. I can't think what else would have got me delving inside a book with a cover image of a white-robed man waving from his popemobile. I am so glad I did though; the poetry was like nothing I had ever come across. It took a while to build up to reading whole poems – after a line or two I would want to lie down or stare out of a window … so concentrated was the meaning, so targeted at the 'real Self', this was poetry supremely designed to steer the weary, searching soul Godwards, and it quite literally had the effect, on me anyway, of knocking the wind out of my sails.

I did not decide to follow Jesus until some time later, and then not from within the Roman Catholic tradition, but my love of Wojtyła's poetry and my desire to tell people about his remarkable verse continues. I am surprised, and somewhat dismayed, how little known it is, amongst Roman Catholics, as well as those from other Christian traditions. It is well-documented that Wojtyła had a deep interest in literature and wrote poetry and plays, but serious scholarship, and an attempt to place his writing within contemporary poetics, has not been forthcoming.

But even to identify why not is instructive. Perhaps it is in part to do with what Professor Dybciak identifies in his essay *The Poetic Phenomenology of a Religious Man: About the Literary Creativity of Karol Wojtyła*: 'In today's literary culture an anti-generic and *eo ipso* anti-biographical current predominates … We focus our attention on the works themselves, assuming that they contain everything the author wants to tell us. But in the present instance we must depart from that rule.' Wojtyła's biography absolutely towers over his literary work, and a serious literary study would necessitate departing from this *eo ipso* trend, where something is understood only in terms of itself.

I would say that the trend in modern aesthetics to separate the author from their writing, or the work of art from the artist who created it, is just plain wrong. If there is to be a Christian aesthetic of the arts, then I believe the two must be brought back together – otherwise we are falling prey to the impersonal Hegelian historicist error that says a work of art is a creation, not a reflection, a monument and not a document. Benedetto Croce, considered by some to be the father of modern aesthetics, said in his *Aesthetica in Nuce*: 'What matters is not what the poet proposes or believes to make, but only what he has actually made.' This strongly Historicist position is in many ways the equal opposite to the Personalist philosophy that so deeply influenced Wojtyła's life and thought.

Personalism asserts that the real is the personal, that the basic features of man's personality form the pattern of all reality. In the theistic form that Personalism has often assumed, and certainly in Wojtyła's case, it sometimes becomes specifically Christian, holding that not merely the person but the highest individual instance of personhood – Jesus Christ – is the pattern. So for Wojtyła the artist is as important as the work of art they produce, and it is the very thought, intention and deepest desire of the artist that communicates, or speaks through, the work of art, and imbues it with value and significance.

In these days of Tracy Emin's bed and Damian Hurst's diamond-encrusted skull, I would encourage any aspiring or practicing artist to read Pope John Paul II's *Letter to Artists*. He clearly desired to encourage craftsmen and women whose activity he considered to mirror the image of the Creator, as people uniquely gifted to positively 'form the spirit of society and of peoples'. It is clear to me from this letter that Wojtyła would have agreed with Shakespeare that art is a deeply personal reflection and document, and not as Croce expressed it, an impersonal creation and monument. Shakespeare encapsulation of the mission of theatre, may be equally said of other art forms: 'Its end both at the first and now, was and is, to hold, as 'twere the mirror up to nature; to show virtue her own feature, scorn her own image, and the very age and body of time his form and pressure.'

Wojtyła's writings on theatre contain a rare depth of insight into the whole realm of the arts. His *Collected Plays and Writing on Theatre* is long out-of-print, as it most of Wojtyła's literary work, and extremely expensive to get hold of. I found a copy in the stacks of Columbus' University Library in New York City and photocopied the essays … I was transfixed to read of his approach; it is the same approach that I see in his poetry - namely that problem solving is central. He says in *On the Theater of the Word*: 'The problem acts … The impact of the performance is caused not by events, transferred in a literary manner from life to the stage, but by the problem itself.' His most well-known play *The Jeweller's Shop* presents a problem devastating in its impact if no solution is found. I would state the problem like this: How can marriage be wanted or desirable if you have grown up a/ with only the ghost of a father or b/ within the ego-driven bitterness of parents in flight from themselves and the world?

And what of the problems posed in Wojtyła's poetry? Death, our deepest dilemma, needs to be accepted as an inevitable reality. Wojtyła writes in *Song of a Hidden God / Shores of Silence* (1944): 'In such silence I hide, / A leaf released from the wind, / No longer anxious for the days that fall. / They must all fall, I know.' He tells the girl let down in love: 'You think you are the centre of things. If only you could grasp that you are not. / The centre is He, / And He too finds no love - / Why don't you see?' To the schizoid he says: 'You must give heart space to your moments / Space to the pressure of will.' And to the Melancholic his advise is: 'Push aside the terror of things to be done, / May a simple act be enough.'

As well as poetry with a sharp pastoral focus, much of Wojtyła's verse encodes the mystical experience within a system of contemporary poetics. I don't know of anyone else apart from St John of the Cross who has done this so 'perfectly'. Professor Dybciak in the same essay I quoted from earlier, mirrors the soul's journey in Wojtyła's poetry with the stages mapped out by St John of the Cross, so providing us with a valuable interpretative tool. The stages are: water of life, the inner and outer night, solitary suffering, the vision of the soul, opening consciousness and space, incomplete knowledge, the divine light and communion.

So where does this journey take us? Wojtyła says in his poem cycle *The Church,* 'Though you see no abyss in the mind / Don't imagine it is not there'. Too many of us these days are busy avoiding the abyss – the place where we stand exposed to who we really are. And if we can bear to tarry in that place a while, there opens up the possibility of seeing God as He really is. And then we cannot but encounter Christ …

Many of the poems in this collection show forth the willingness of their authors to go on such a journey inwards, and that is to be highly commended indeed. Art that is born out of the contemplative life of the artist brings with it the possibility of engendering contemplation in the 'beholder'. So much of what passes as art today, and so much in contemporary culture, overwhelms the senses, instead of doing what art should do when it is welded to true spirituality, namely free a person from the activism that overwhelms their inner, spiritual nature. Wojtyła's poetry certainly did this for me.

I will conclude with Wojtyła's words from *Letter to Artists* as a reminder of the high calling of artists who are Christians: 'It is up to you, men and women who have given your lives to art, to declare with all the wealth of your ingenuity that in Christ the world is redeemed: the human person is redeemed, the human body is redeemed, and the whole creation which, according to Saint Paul, 'awaits impatiently the revelation of the children of God' (Romans 8 v. 19), is redeemed. The creation awaits the revelation of the children of God also through art and in art. This is your task. Humanity in every age, and even today, looks to works of art to shed light upon its path and its destiny.'

Sarah Fordham, May 2011

HEARTSPEAK: A CONTEMPLATIVE CHORUS

I: PERSON AND ACT

I want to show you the contours of my life

To shine a light on the caves
Explain to you my boulders
Sing to you my lakes
Sparkle to you my highways
And illuminate my scars

I want to show you the contours of my life
The things I have been through
The wars I have battled
The victory and bloodshed
So you can see i've earnt the medal

I want you to see that I did it for love
I want you to see that God helped me through
The moments of triumph
The depths of gloom
From caverns and depths
From hell and flames
To soar on clouds and high streams
With angels and water seams

Anna Verey

[The] Priest-Machine

[I was made for this.] All is artifice
— the cylinder-sinew, the gold soldered skin, the ticking organs, the viscera of cogs.

Decorated with the emboss of tritons and fountainheads
I am the soul, steel sharp, heavy with the thud of blank movement.
Oiled with chrism. [I was made for this.]

The unction stone is set in precise geometry. Dribbled marble and power
latent in the accoutrements. This is altar.

A swaying alb in crimson nylon, cribbed colours of a haemograph.
Thirty-seven reds. A spell of charred resin, the smoke tearing the air.
Bread.
[thaumaturge-engine] turning lipped [moisture] into {YHWH}

Gabriel Olearnik

Believe

Does being not surprise you?
For what cause are you here?
Do you feel God's living presence?
Do you yearn for things so dear?

Is there hope in your silence?
For a sure and well-worn path?
How to find and keep the secret?
Where on earth is joy and love?

Are you tired of old excuses?
Puzzled by a painful health?
Do you worry, ponder, wander?
Are you restless in your wealth?

Where resides your inner longing?
Is your smile a sign of peace?
Who loves you now, has always?
Who abides without release?

Why is more never enough?
When I die why was I born?
Who or what made me to think?
Do I live or breathe forlorn?

Why the signs of wondrous nature?
Where the reason for the questions?
Who is sacred, loving, true?
Why can't I see, yet wish so to do?

Is my guilt a mark of Law?
Human strivings empty, poor?
Why the same, again, all dust?
What is Passion, what is lust?

Am I human or mere creature?
Do I know life's task of trust?
Why the darkness, fear of death?
When will grace propel my faith?

Piotr Stolarski

The Wasted Tree

God said, 'Enjoy the Sacred Tree!

Don't consume it,

Let it be.

Contemplate the fruit-filled bough
Wonder at beauty, bless and bow,

Reverence its inviolate charms
And leave in peace from the grasping arms

The Tree that exists for its sake alone
Not to be a victim of the take and own.'

But Eve attended to the Serpent's lie
'It costs you nothing,
Come and buy, for free, what God withholds from you,
He said you'd die. It isn't true.

This tree is wasted.

Use it up!

Fill your empty knowledge cup.

'Good and Evil you don't know,
But eat the fruit and how you'll grow,
Into Gods
Come on
You'll see.
Only gods eat from the Wasted Tree.'

'Ooh says Eve, d'you think I should?
Still you're right,
It does look good.'

Now kept out of Eden by a flaming sword,
The serpent is as true

As his slippery word
For now, consuming night and day
Good and evil come our way
And Eden, where Mankind could play
Becomes the sweat-toil of today.

The Sacred Tree was raped of fruit
We rape the world in a pure wool suit.
And violate the Sacred Day
The Sabbath that was made for prayer and play.

Sacred, useless, life-filled Tree
Save us from Efficiency!

But lo! I hear the sound of feet
Hurrying, scurrying to compete.
The Wasted tree of Life they seek
To make a good story for 'Start the Week'.

The intellectual appetite needs
New thrills that old religion feeds.

Designer ideas to fill the mind
Out on the airwaves, tuned refined,
No thought unturned, left undefined
Packaged and marketed, PR entwined.

Sacred, useless, Life-filled Tree
Pulped to fiction for the BBC.

What leaf of life can I find of you
That might instruct us what to do?
What leaf-fringed legend might I find
En-treasured in the poet's mind?

Sap of spirit, silent voice
We cannot undo the choice

Good and evil we received when the serpent we believed.

Adam lost the Tree of Life
Though complicit, blamed his wife.

Exile we cannot undo,
But the Sacred filters through
Evil we cannot unknow
But can we let the wasted grow?

Can we listen for the silent sound
Root inviolate
Underground
Simply living
Growing yet
He who heard
Could not forget

Sacred, Life-filled, Sabbath Free
Shelter us, Oh Sacred Tree!

Sarah de Nordwall

our love is like

your love is like a bridge
taking me to the city
a place teeming with life
and prosperity
not danger and poverty

my love is like a swallow
flitting here and there
sometimes seen, sometimes not
sometimes singing, sometimes silent
but always returning

Sarah Fordham

MY PRAYER

NOW – Raise the mind and heart to God.
Come – Raise up mind,
Come – Raise up heart,
Let's dance together before the Lord.

But oh how hard.
The mind just twists and turns
Seeking always a distraction.
No dancing here,
Only the plod of very random thoughts.

You dancing heart. The very centre of my being,
Where is your song?
Where gone your flying feet.-
Just sit this out,
And let the time drag on.

Listen. - A new tune,
Has touched the edge of my perception.
A vibrant form is dancing in the ring.
The music swells, it touches mind and heart;
It beckons; draws me ever close to Him.

So then together we;
My Father God, my brother Jesus too;
The Spirit leading joins up every part.
The heart cries out,
The mind with joy responds.
The very body, bowing low
Gets up to join the reel.

The music fades, my partner slips away,
But in his going
Leaves behind a resting spirit.
A mind that's now at ease,
A heart that's full,
Of God's own benediction.

Michael Hoare

The gatekeeper

Always there are two ways.
The first, over wall or roof,
brings forth no truth.
I can only control.
Suspicion takes hold.

Always there are two ways.
The second, by the door,
brings forth more.
I lose control.
Love takes hold.

Always there are two ways.
By the door, a figure waits,
Through whom I journey
to the distant shore.
His love restores.

Jonathan Fordham

GRASSLAND TO GRACELAND

These little black letters you read,
Are like little black lambs and sheep, foraging for blank spaces.
Are you a neutral observer, a greasy sheep spotter, a wolf, a freak?
Lost in the woods looking for leaves?
Are you a veggie, a meat eater?
Is it spiritual food you seek?
Are you sick of too much searching?
Just asking!
Don't pull wool over your eyes.
Rather find in these fields goodness for you to feed.
God is the best doctor,
Best chef and dietician.
He wants to make you, his heir, whole,
Shine, and iron out your crisis.
God can come in a bush or as The Lamb, as He wishes.
Even in a piece of bread, with no frill
Irony of being fully air and Graces,
He can also be in the harvester
And his breath in the breeze, for the windmill.
He is the one in whom all get fulfilled.

Grown from seeds in diverse circumstances,
Every pages are filled with nutritious words, ideas and Graces,
Planted, nourished and looked after by the best gardener there is.
They are never there to force-feed you like geese.
But they befit misfits, to their own benefit,
Also God geeks,
And all of us, God's kids.

With a little authorised excentricity,
Find in this anthology divine authority,
Fine authorship in apologetic stylee,
No duplicity, just authenticity

Jean Hubert

The Loving Gene
(for Richard Dawkins)

As atheist to my theist I was interested to meet you,
To ask the anti to my thesis how can truth
Be measured in a test tube or abstract mathematical rule?
But there's no time in business for God, or love,
So instead I made you tea as you padded round the room in your socks,
Checking proofs, not the scientific kind, hard copy only.
You were distant as you settled down, polite, reserved,
Efficient in your speech and movements.
I wondered, were you thinking of your kids?
Would you telephone out when no one was listening
To tell your wife how much you love her?

Looking back I wish I'd asked you where you think
The light that shines in darkness comes from,
From where the grace that holds this world together,
From whom the poor and suffering and oppressed draw strength?
The old eternal questions that leave us quaking in our shoes –
How little, or how much, do they mean to you?
Did you sweat with fear and dread to come to your position?
Yet I simply handed you your tea and asked
If there was anything you needed. You said not.
The space between our worlds stretched several galaxies.
I think, therefore I am. Descartes said that.
I am loved by God, therefore I love. I said that.

Jonathan Fordham

Raphael

One of the brothers says
That old nun is a dear, but
So dotty that when you talk with her
It's like falling
Into a tumble dryer.

A little while back I headed up the M1 to see her,
Windscreen wipers battling
This vale of tears.

So I was glad to be
Warmed up,
Spun round,
And gently tipped out
On the other side of reality.

Fr Dominic White, OP

Post-modern prayer

My heart is a shattered mirror
which almost reflects your face.

If only I could piece together enough fragments
to catch a glimpse of your eyes
and be sure of their constant, smiling welcome.

Don't be afraid, blind heart.
Wait in the darkness
and I will gather together each splinter
until smudged with painstaking blood
you see me again
and your cracks resolve in my reflection.

1998?

Catherine Cruz, FMVD

Space-time in the Suburbs

Paris is without doubt one of the most elegant and beautiful cities in the world. But even Paris has some boring suburbs! Yet God is everywhere, and even a dull place can be transformed by real art. A month ago I went to Wissous in the southern burbs to see a performance by Lambert Vadrot (stage name Pravarshan), a French Indian dancer who is profoundly rooted in his relationship with Christ and his training in classical Indian dance. When he dances, Lambert understands that he's making an offering of himself, and what he gives to the audience is what he has received from God. Here's what I experienced with Lambert and his dance ensemble.

Space-time in the Suburbs

Another faceless suburbanity
("Where clichés become reality")
The style of the houses perhaps a little different
But here too boredom defaces the timetable
Of the residual bus service,
Which is the last gasp of metaphysics
On the billionth empty Saturday
In the history of the world.

The arts centre has the same seating
As you might see anywhere, bright, flexible and linkable
From Wissous to East Wimbledon
Sutton to Sénart.
(They've made enough to run the length of the Channel Tunnel:
Now that would be advertising.)
It's not out of a French film,
Existential Gaulloises and femmes fatales.
Still, perhaps it's the fortune
Of a canny businessman
Sneered at for being nouveau riche,
Then meeting idealism, suddenly opening his heart
That made all this possible tonight.

And does it matter really whether it's Wimbledon or Wissous
When he danced, Shiva baptised and untamed
Destroying cynical boredom,
Cruelty and gaping voids

In minutes
Which reach eternity?
Space-time's only a cliché
If you've not been there
In Wissous or Wimbledon (East), it doesn't matter
How ordinary or extraordinary the stage
Danced by a man who dares to be humble,
Vision glorious.

Fr Dominic White, OP

God, you have made a cruel world

The sun is shining and the fields are lush,
But brambles crush us with thorns of prison ivy
Juicy black berries drip sweet blood onto our eyeballs
Prevent us from seeing.

What is man, that he could be?
A marvellous shining creature of light and smile
Yet each a universe banished to live alone
Icicles gripping onto each other for fear of falling
Grasping each others legs tightly and screaming,
"don't let go! Don't let go! Loneliness will be King if you fall!"

Loneliness has long reigned and every day the storm comes to a close and
Exiled to his own bed
Thoughts of majesty and dreams of could-be
Throw daggers at our flesh and beg on the streets.

"Help me!" They cry,
To become more than I am
They sit on the side of pavement, huddled in a corner, hands outstretched.
Dust and dirt darkening their faces,
"Help me become more than I am!"

Begging for money they hope will build the mansion that will be the home of song and sunlight they long for.
They collect and collect, yet each mansion falls.
Time and effort are spent, potential expended
Dreams offered and pawned.
Yet the bricks won't build
The beams don't meet

Dreams sob quietly,
Not wanting to disturb those pouting and perusing in bustling cafes.
They sob.
Sitting together in a corner, a group of dreams get together and play chess, their dusty tweed coats smiling as they brush one another's elbows. Their stomachs are full and sweetly satisfied but nobody comes to pick them up.

Like old men needing companions, with good but fatal humour, they wait.

Who will ever collect them, see their beauty and take them and make them a home?
They live forever but without a companion, their pain thickens and wounds of war
Explode blood onto the other customers.

Nobody wants them now and the shocked faces of coffee drinkers keep speculative distance safely.
Alone they remain.
Alone forever, sleeping and crying, wishing and dying,
In royal blood.

Anna Verey

Anatomy

Speak then heart, beating in my breast,
I lend to you my tongue, my mouth, my breath.
The rain began to fall upon my head;
Grieving for someone who was not dead, but
Alive, grieving for their life, their presence,
Not their death, their going hence, their absence.

Andrew Thornton-Norris

Byzantium

Such an abyss between the words and the intent,
the gulf of possible lives and action
dark it is, the future, the future.
I make it with my hands like a man
bridging a precipice, mud bricks on the parapets.
The gamble of my life.

I have loved these calf-lands. The pastures fat and black.
I make sacrifices to the god of spaces
people do not understand.
The cattle burn in the ridges,
the Golden Horn incensed with meat
and a bronze knife trimmed with bull blood
shouts for heaven's mercy. (The answer is unheard.)

I make sacrifices to the spaces in myself
my hopes watered. These streets will not be as I saw them
for the blind are building my city. Perhaps it is enough
that the city stands at all. Water on three sides.
Poseidon will ward us against the tumult of history.
Death and war will touch our walls, but not carry them.

Here will stand subjects and emperors
on this lip of cusped continents.

I had forgotten the purpose of exhaustion
and the god of spaces does not answer.

Gabriel Olearnik

Wisdom of the wayside....

By the wayside Lord,
there's commotion and a crowd rushes.
I haven't managed to keep up,
so here I am,
by the wayside.
You see my legs don't work as they should.
Weak, unable to run.
Blind to the world- I can only sit
by the wayside.

I once saw clearly, but now lids have swollen
light doesn't reach the pupil.
Others can pass and dodge what comes.
I can't see, so it's safer to sit by the wayside.

But here Lord, I'm left out
Can't join in, can't run, so the crowd passes by.
But blindness has advantages
I hear well and have time,
precious time to think and pray,
as I sit by the wayside.
It doesn't make up for the helplessness I feel,
but it gives me time to prepare my call
to the figure that approaches and causes unusual noise,
commotion of an undaily kind.
Hear whisperings, "it's Him"
I've heard of Him.
So wait and sense His timing,
close now,
nearer,
ready,
nearly,
just gone by,
now,
"Son of David, have pity on me."

This is what the wayside has prepared me for.
Given me faith, humility to call and keep on calling.
He will hear, because I believe.

He will heal and let me see
if I only ask.

The wayside prepared me to ask.
To ask from the depths, to the only Saviour there is.
To put me in the truth, before our powerful God,
that we are all blind and need our King
to restore our hearts and let our lips sing
His praise and to follow.
All who hear the praise from my lips
will then praise too and learn the wisdom of the wayside.

Kate Golding

The End of the World

For Sarah de Nordwall, Bard Fondatrice

Cheer up, it's the
End of the World!
It only comes once a year.
Behold, I looked down
From the cosmic bathroom
Up in the Northern Heights:
I saw the world at peace
In the final harmony of
Starlight and streetlight.
But what length (will you say?) some people go to with their platitudes,
poetic in their splendid isolation and blind to the lies, the cries, the endless
stress and mess of conflicts great and small, unlit by star- or streetlight,
unheeded and unhealed suffering that makes this world? You only need
cross this city's breadth, western hopes of Heathrow suddenly crushed in
microspace of hypertime across a tissue of moments passed (is your art any
more than a hunt for highs?), arriving only to depart again from the higher
rents of a dream and its garden in Hackney in the east.
But then I changed at King's Cross, stopped running seeking hiding falling
Bowed my head
And marvelled
Under its lightness
This place where
One foresuffered all
Here at last.
And, though pain will come
As pain must
And dull incomprehension
Makes pain from pain (again)
Yet I am here
How strangely good it is
To descend into more
Still communion.
This beauty's given
Itself and lovely
Because it's no more my god.

And the Queen of the South
Will arise, wise
In shot-up Streatham
And astonish and exalt them
With her peace greater than
A Saturday stabbing.
They prefer to dance now,
And the commuters, wandering poets,
Write the light from the bridge
Where the crazy Blackfriars
Are building a station big enough.
Here you are at last,
Now in reality's welcome depths
Where Adam lies, ready to rise, here, at the end of the world.

Fr Dominic White, OP

Fish caught in prison

Break down the walls of my prison
Let me see loving come shining in.
Let me find forgiveness,
Where there was sin;
Let the best world begin.

The love I crave hurts me more
As there are no fish to catch the hook.
My days in agony,
Writhing and caught
Nothing broken
Nothing bought.
Shattered pain,
Awkward fear,
Please God, get me out of here.

With every text I write,
Hoping to find some respite, from my loneliness.
Can you read the question in my lines?
Can you feel the pain and the prize?
In anguish and pain,
Let me start my life again,
I don't want to waste a single hour but
Bloom perfectly like a spring flower.

Anna Verey

CHOOSE FREEDOM

I learnt shame in childhood
and my undernourished heart
developed the habit for decades.
"It's your fault" became my fault,
and in the confusion
knee-jerk reactions became
easier than measured reflections.

I walled in my inadequacies :
I achieved goals
with energy and strength.
Then I grew old.
'Give me time for amendment of life'
urges a Collect in the prayer book.
We are never too old to see
through our self deceptions
to the heart of the matter.

When my hopes lie in tatters,
panic prevails: I hear
the 'blame game' ceaselessly rolling
as I roll in the pit
and the pit of my stomach ulcerates.
How can I escape
the pain of this place?
I breathe, breathe life
and air into the tension.

I remember a wise old friar
saying, lovingly:
'God looks at the intentions of our hearts,
not the mess we make of our lives.'

Helen de Borchgrave

Seeds of Gold

Hear the silence
Listen to your heart beat
Dust the cobwebs
Enter in those places
That you try to avoid, to block away
Open those doors you have the key
Let the light in, draw the curtains
Wide back, wide back…

Don't build with lies, you've got to try
To seek your face under the sun
To get the smile back in your eyes

THERE'S MAGIC THERE FOR YOU
IT WILL TURN WHAT YOU'VE GONE THROUGH
INTO SEEDS OF GOLD, THOSE SEEDS CAN GLOW
THOSE SEEDS WILL GROW!

Touch your hardness
Scratch the rusty surface
Open windows
Blow the dust around you
Into clouds that rise and fill the air
Got to be brave, you've got to wait
Cause the time will make the light shine
Through them, through them

Don't hide the pain, don't be afraid
To seek the truth speaking of you
To find the mirror of your soul

THERE'S MAGIC THERE FOR YOU
IT WILL TURN WHAT YOU'VE GONE THROUGH
INTO SEEDS OF GOLD, THOSE SEEDS CAN GLOW
THOSE SEEDS WILL GROW!

Seeds of gold, seeds of truth, seeds of life…
Those seeds will grow…
Seeds of gold

Paula Jordao, FMVD

Last Night

I walked in the world when it was new,
no more than swirls of atoms on a dark
eternal nothing. God leaned down, whispered:
'This is my vision: there will be mountains,
plains, rivers, seas. There will be summers,
winters. I will make seeds, give rain and sun
to grow trees, flowers, grass so creatures
of every kind can evolve. I will make men
and women with minds and hearts to love
this world and all that is in it and they will
love me.' I said: 'God, this will be beautiful.'

I walked in the world. Men and women lived
in fear. They hated each other and everything
around them. They'd turned their backs on God.
I wept. God leaned down, spoke another vision:
'I will give the world my only son, a part of me
they can know and, knowing, love. And yet,
I see him despised, murdered so I will use
that atrocity to turn the people back to me.
They'll see my love and long for me when
I say: "I forgive."' I said: 'God, your love
is beautiful, it overwhelms us.'

I walked in the world. Some parts were good,
some parts were bad, some people loved, some
people hated, some were too bored to care. I saw
the land scarred, polluted, excrement poured
into rivers and seas, and yet I dreamed a world
of exuberant new life, men and women living
in harmony, loving God, praising God. Then
God leaned down, said: 'You have dreamed
well. Now, go out, make it real.'

Kaye Lee

Nine Lives

Once I believed in history
Once I believed in time
Once I believed in people
Once I called all things mine

Twice I believed in power
Twice I believed in control
Twice I believed in change
By means of violent overthrow

Three times I loved my woman
Three times I gave her my best
Three times she took it smiling
And put it away with the rest

Four times I worked for the Man
Four times I swore under my breath
Four times I counted my money
Yet owed every penny that was left

Five times I dug the land
Five times I planted seed
Five times I grew food
And felt self-sufficient indeed

Six times I helped my neighbour
Six times I gave him my bed
Six times the scoundrel pissed in it
Until I shut my door in his face instead

Seven times I made speeches
Seven times my language was charged
Seven times I won the argument
Seven times my pride enlarged

Eight times I went to war
Eight times I took up arms
Eight times I was defeated
And left to rely on my charms

Nine times I explored religion
Nine times I tried to ‘deep breathe’
Nine times I practised meditation
Nine times I was deceived

Once I followed a stranger
Once I gave everything away
Once I let go of my life

Jonathan Fordham

THE HEART

You called us out to step into your heart.
To make that journey from the place we sat,
Into a new unknown where we had never been.
Not one by one, each person making his own stand,
But all together; Community
Called into the heart of Christ.

Some hurry forth,
Eager to answer to that urgent call.
Others more slowly, fearful to feel the fool;
And some reluctant, lest their own heart break.
"Christ is this you? Or just a big mistake."

At last we all are in this fragile place.
Holding each other in a close embrace.
Raising our voices and our tears in praise.
Not yet we know;
But slow our minds with light, see a new mystery
Hidden but so bright
That we in love together ARE THE HEART OF CHRIST.

Michael Hoare

II: LORD AND LIFEGIVER

House of Bread*

Wise men, take off your wisdom
and leave it outside
in the darkness of the streets
of Bethlehem.

Giants, bow down your heads
in case you wound them
on the mantle of the doorway
of the House of Bread.

Kings, cast down your crowns
best not to clutter
the little temple
of the Son of God.

Martin Earle

**Bet Lechem* are the Hebrew words for House of Bread

Push aside the Terror of Things to be Done*

Push aside the terror of things to be done;
They were deceivers, ever.
They catch at you without context
Claiming territory
Without treaty
On Sacred ground.

Push aside the terror of things calling
Clamouring from the four corners
Claiming the floor
Where He had brought you to dance
To laugh, To sing, With Him
Alone.

But the things
trip you
They know that appeasement
knocks you
On your slight shins.
And your lack of stature in your own estimation
Has put you on higher heels
Than the dance requires.

And you trip early
Before the music plays.

And the terror of things falling
Reminds you
There is so much to clear away
To do away with
To run away from
Before the night Falls.

Push aside the terror of things to be done
For the blind beggar is calling
He is calling out to the Son of David
Whom he cannot see
But whom he knows, he hears
Is passing by.

And the wild clamour of his ardent anguish
Cannot be smothered
By the hostile crowd.

He is losing hope at the terror of people crushing him
But the Master stops
For him alone
And tells him to
Draw near.

And the crowd turns to the seated man
“Courage, Bartimeus,
He is calling you”
And the cloak that protects him
He flings aside
And he runs
In his personal darkness
 to the Lord Who waits.

Push aside the terror of things to be done
There is nothing to be done
 but to hear Him
 asking
“What do you want of me?”
The One by whom all things can be done.

And the beggar,
Wise, in his reckless trust
Begs now for the gift of sight.
And Jesus, son of David
Has pity on him
And says “Go” for the Light has come –
“Your faith has healed you”
The dark has gone
And his eyes receive the sun.

And Bartimeus accompanies Him
Along the road
At once.
The terror at last is pushed aside.
The winter is over

And gone.

Sarah de Nordwall

*Inspired by the title of a poem (of the same title) by Pope John Paul II and Fr Antonio's sermon on Bartimeus

Quiet Time

I'm much too busy for an hour, Lord!
An hour of … being with you.

Do you really want to see me, Lord?
I could spare 5 minutes.

Well you did ask me to serve you
So, I'm serving you – 24 hours a day.

An hour, Lord. What about 10 minutes?

*   *   *

Cathedral is quiet, away from the crowds
But what will I do for an hour, Lord?

Nothing. Nothing! I can't afford an hour
of nothing. Can I? Well, don't know, Lord.

Must make a note for Anne, and buy some bread
on the way home … Hello. Lord.

Are you there? If I don't talk, you could talk
Lord. Can you help me? … Please.

It's getting more peaceful in the silence

*   *   *

Lord, it's good not to have to plan
Just sit in your Presence and gaze

Perhaps I could come again?
Tomorrow?

Jacqui Houlihan

God is Love

Love is the most beautiful thing in the world!
It is this deep warm hand that reaches into the truth of what we are.

A touch that hears the unspoken thought,
the unfelt emotion
It sees all things, knows all things

Perceives more than the person of its attention
Oh wonderful Love!
How I need your touch!
To hear me, to welcome me,

to embrace the me that is unknown to myself.

Help me rest in your gaze
Help me welcome your presence
Unabashed and unashamed
To revel in your joy!
Your gift, your self
And to find my self through you.
Love allows the other to speak
Enables the other to reveal itself freely

And in its waiting draws more out than a hundred questions could attain.

Kate Golding

On the Way of the Cross

Kissed but betrayed
Followed but denied
Judged by your words
Judged by their lies
You were accused, you were despised,
You were condemned under their trial
You were insulted, you were mocked
With no mercy with no right

But your unshaken trust
And your doubtless faith
Led you on the way of the cross
Slowly you rise
Step by step you walk
You fall but you arise
Until all, is fulfilled in you

Helped but oppressed
Mourned but not freed
Loaded with your cross
Loaded with their sins
You were rejected and disowned
You were accursed under their Law
You were determined and resolved
You knew there was no other way
Cause your unshaken trust
And your doubtless faith
Led you on the way of the cross
Slowly you rise
Step by step you walk
You fall but you arise
Until all, is fulfilled in you
Today as you breathe your last…

Paula Jordao, FMVD

ENEMY PARADE

Identity parade helps to name thy enemy
He's at war and enduring, don't thou cry victory
Nor do rest on thy laurel, he's a weed much too hardy
He won't the hatchet bury and this is no comedy.

Sataniel became Satan, separated from Elohim
Won't be absolved, it's too late, wants to believe he's winning
The absolute renegade leads others to suffering

This is no happy ballad, all in all a true story
With no gun, no blade, no run, but the running blood of Thee
Who was killed at thirty-three, to get rid of him for thee
To save thou through thy faith and worship Thee in glory

Jean Hubert

Empty of Nothing
(For Thomas J.J. Altizer)

Thomas says that He has died
Emptying Himself for others
A Spirit in our times, spreading
A suicidal God despairing

Of His own creation
Of the scope of evil
Of His own loving power
A projection of lost souls

But You are not Dead, or death
Just Lord and servant God!
Height in lowliness
Living Servant-Lord of Israel!

You have full life, and are not dead
After resurrection and ascent
You are my life, my love in action
My heart is full, of thee for me

Kenosis is to *be alive* for others
Empty of a deathly void seducing
Full in Spirit with incarnate joy
My God Is All in All that hopes

Immanent,
Transcendent,
The Holy One!

Piotr Stolarski

A PRAYER OF ABANDONMENT

In your presence Lord;
In the wonder of your glory, I am lost.
Blinded by your radiance, in this bright darkness,
I give myself to you,
Knowing that only here, without my sight
Can you be seen and I can truly live.

Father, truth and only certainty.
The gift of this my being do I return to you.
Receive these blinded eyes, that I may see.
This tongue, struck dumb, tear from my mouth;
That in your hands it will your praises sing.
These ears that oft have listened in vain,
Fill now with the music of your Word.

My hands, my feet, my body. These are yours.
Each tumbled thought, each impulse of my tangled being,
Cry out to you my God;
Take this my mutilated gift,
That once you gave in beauty
And such generous, glorious perfection.

This heart, my love, reach out and take.
Mould it dear Master, once more into that likeness,
Which pierced and broken yours had been.
Mine petrified, but not yet stone,
May still bleed into the likeness of your own.

And last my Father dear, this soul I leave;
Sullied, besmirched into your care.
Misshapen from this life excess of greed and lust;
Abandoned by me, take it Lord for it is yours.
That you may alter and complete it
Into a likeness of your beloved Son.

Michael Hoare

The Mystic Body

To thee I give a gift freely bought
Not of labour nor of pain but love
So that our two flesh may be one
Our souls together in the sacred garden
The snake of selfishness banished therefrom
As each one's self is given for the other
Naked and without shame in ecstasy
As in the liturgy of love we see
The light that is beyond is also here

Andrew Thornton-Norris

WATER BLUE

Life with colour is never bland
When God speaks, his words are blue

You can not count each drop in an ocean
But you can grab one or two if you really try to
And don't you keep it just for you,
Away from others, out of view
Your blue droplet belongs to all around
Close your eyes and imagine all it can do
You just left Holyhead towards Ireland
You notice droplets at low tide
Milling around the sand that sits tight
Imagine what they do deeper down
For the algaes, the plancton
For the Gulfstream, in the Atlantic
Its effect on the climate
How it carries icebergs from the Arctic
Let it be part of it and freeze
Let it take Titanics and dreams
Let it shape coastlines and river streams
Let it boil in a kettle, become steam
Let it go and feed mists and clouds
Let it go on grass, be dew
Let it fill animal in troughs
Barrels in local brews
Let it clean us in wash basins
In our muscles and tissues
Let it please fishes and dolphins
Let it do what it's meant to be doing
Or have an identity crisis
A drop of sweat falls from your forehead
Back into the sea near Holyhead
Open your eyes, enjoy the view
The sand is white, the sky is blue
Damn! How long I've been in the desert?
How long to accept the truth?
I need the well of Madam Samaritan.
Have you, God, yet not discerned,
That I deserve your fresh water to make my heart anew?

Now I feel a droplet on my cheek
A tear!
A sign from me to you

Life with colour is never bland
When God speaks, his words are blue

Jean Hubert

The Door

How to extract
The still centre of thought,

when time is a line
running back and forth

spilling through my hands
like sand upon the ground?

If you gave me a vein of gold,
would I spin from the seam

fine cloth as a garment
to cover my naked wound,

or would I make myself an altar
as an offering to the world?

My hands are empty, outstretched.
I will carry the world in my arms.

My lips move ceaselessly,
forming unknown words.

Time is gathered up,
eternity becoming moment's measure.

In my mind's eye, a door.
I knock. Then enter.

Jonathan Fordham

WHICH WORLD?

'Do not forget there are two worlds.

Let the bondage of this one fall away
and come deeper into my world.
The way is blocked
by your fears and anxieties,
blinded by your defence mechanisms.
Give them to me, one by one,
give them again and again,
as gifts –
in return for my grace.

To enter my green pastures
just listen - with an open heart
Gradually in the silence,
clarity will come.

I opened the door
when I died on the Cross.
Follow in faith,
as I lead you to freedom:
freedom from the dark cell of self,
freedom from the sins of the fathers.
Accept the pain as I heal those wounds
that oppress you.
This takes time - like all growth.

The world grows dark and confused,
teeming with people
streaming through life with their heads down;
missing my light, refusing
my offer of love.

As you listen to me,
I listen to you.
Rejoice with those blessed ones
who experience salvation;
who move beyond the cares of this world

into the wide open space
of peace and detachment -
of inexpressible joy
in the inner world,
where I am.’

Helen de Borchgrave

Desirous (for Christian unity)

I want to see You

Here, now, forever

I want to love You, truly

Daily, patiently, giving

Trying to comprehend by not under-standing, clearly

In faith transcending immanence, outside – within, transcendence

You are Holy, Spirit, Lord-God, height and depth

You emptied You to be like me, like us, east and west

Then died to save to Love, to live, with us, in us, sacred

Your Word is holy, Your Face is holy, Your Blood is holy

Lamb, child, God, balm, bread

Everything You are and show is Love for me

Each truth is a piercing for my heart, for free

Do You know how much I love you? How much I want to love You more?

Stay and be You, with us

Lord, brother, father, spirit, friend

JESUS

Stay...

Piotr Stolarski

The path of perfection

I love the house where you dwell
As I walk the path of perfection
That yields its fruit in due season.
Turn your ear, pay heed to me
Since you know my longing
To pierce the mysteries of God

In your great love answer me God
In your own house I would dwell
If only the beloved heard my longing.
I cry with all my strength for perfection.
In your great power answer me
With a discerning mind to turn the season.

Your justice has proclaimed the seasons
We place our hope in you o God
In your mercy set me free
At the place where your glory dwells
On the holy mountain of perfection
Which fills the earth with longing

I am filled with humble longing
Even though I am out of season
And still strive for perfection
That is only known by God
When we dig the deep well
Let peace come to me

I will see if it comes to me
Despite all my longing.
The house where I dwell
Is at the mercy of the seasons
And the hand of almighty God
Whose saving staff is perfection

I believe in the path of perfection
Though I don't know if it's for me
And even now I hear God
Whispering my poor longing

Within my hearts season
And the love in which I dwell.

Tom Bentall

Tender God

Tender Lord, please be tender
fragile
I am
Petals unfolding but
fragile
Thanks for watching
Thanks for not speaking
but loving
no rush
you know my time
I love you
Tender God
I will be yours

Kate Golding

Jacob's Well

Midday sun levels
brittle grass, dry red earth
to a uniform brightness.
Only the well keeps its shadows,
like a memory lined with secrets
harbouring a constant miracle.

A woman comes to draw water.
Dropping her bucket, breaking the silence,
she pulls it back, full and cool.
Giving drink to a stranger,
she spills a flock of brilliant drops,
small wine islands in the dust.

The distant silver circle
holds his darkened face
separate from the day.
The well speaks through him;
she hears for the first time
the running water deep beneath the words.

Catherine Cruz, FMVD

Eph'phatha!

He made me to worship
With soul now aflame
My faith is augmented
Hope points to the gain
I'm feeling no fear
I with Him abide
In my heart I feel Him
His Spirit resides
And when we love each other
Nothing else can appeal
When we share His love
Nothing else is so real
Words are less than silence
The seam deep and hidden
My joy grows greatly now
His presence is unbidden
Knowledge of love is good
But Love Himself is all
Any extraneous object
Results in a heavy fall
From His goodness, for me
In confused acquisition
To hunger assuage
With unreasoned volition
For till now, I was blind
My ears and tongue impaired
Then the Lord whispered 'Open',
And I saw my deep despair
Can I do enough
To have, to use, to be?
Or should I do nothing
Just trust in Him humbly?
Because Jesus is God
His worship my all
Faith, hope, and love
Daily answering the call
I do yearn for You, Lord
For You Are Who You Are
Like no other, Lord Jesus

From up close, from afar
Your glory is boundless
Your justice is sure
Lord God You are gracious
My efforts so poor
Thank You for loving me
Lord Jesus, I pray
May my small, faithful, zeal,
Never wither away

Piotr Stolarski

Missive

Augustine, by the grace of God, bishop
to Ambrose: ordinary of Milan
peace hope and love in the Lord Jesus Christ.

The Psalms say- be of igneous spirits
God kindles the holocaust in my ribs
and my fire burns brightly here in Hippo

There is something greater than the waste
than chaos,
than the burning of the sea
tindered with its spent syllables
torched with words of ash

My friend you have this terrible openness
you read so quietly that I might shout:

Hear me, all the trembling waters
all holy ponds
all wells of art
all pools of poetry

Gilt and bright to harken
in Sadler, Holly, Clerken
The white-words, shining
above the writhe of waters
and the witching of the sea:

(our napalm hearts shall set the world aflame.)

Gabriel Olearnik

Security

I like my security
The sound lock on wild adventures
beyond my tamed dreams
well disguised as a trip
into unknown zones
insured by my credit card

And yet you are beckoning
Hacking the safe code that keeps
my privacy intact
Your magnetic key of love
swipes through all my fears
slashing through my alarmed heart

I like my security
But it is a commodity
overpriced by fears
whilst you pledge free warranty
of insecurity
that covers all my restless life

Monika Chmelova

Prayer of the Unborn

Our dear brothers and sisters,
sons and daughters of the almighty God,
do not forget God's holy prophets:
When God sent messengers to his chosen people to help them to seek and find Him,
they were mocked, stoned and murdered.

And now we, silent prophets of meekness and littleness,
messengers of joy and hope, cry out:
The proud have risen against us,
Ruthless men seek to destroy our lives!

Our elder brothers and sisters,
sons and daughters born of the New Woman, the Church,
do not forget the Saviour of the world!
When, in the fullness of time, God sent us his only Son
He chose as his dwelling the womb of a child and the blessed hiddenness of Nazareth.
And now we, the unborn, the hidden ones,
seek protection and cry out for help!
Speedily rescue us!

Do not forget Jesus our all,
Who became next to nothing for our sake:

Utterly God without beginning or end,
He came to save us by becoming utterly man!

Utterly God in the womb of Mary, as on the hill of Calvary:
He was God Almighty in our human weakness,
Embryo, unborn child, man.

Oh brothers and sisters,
sons and daughters of the living God,
do not forget our Lord!
When He walked among the sons of men, he taught them, saying,
'Whatever you do unto the least of my disciples you do unto me'.
And now we, the unborn, truly the least among you, cry out:
We have been stripped naked – feed us!

We have been deprived of our food – protect us!

Our dear brothers and sisters,
first fruits of the New Creation,
do not forget the waters of your Baptism!
You renounced Satan, all his lies and empty promises,
and so received the Spirit of Truth.
And now we, the unborn, the Holy Innocents, cry out:
Proclaim what is just and right!

And do not forget the Passion of our Lord Jesus Christ!
When he suffered, he did not threaten vengeance
but prayed for those who abused him.
And now we, the unborn, the innocent ones, beseech the Author of all:
'Father forgive them, for truly they do not know what they are doing!'

And do not forget the Holy Eucharist!
When the Eternal King desired to make a dwelling place in passing time
He chose as his host a morsel of bread.
We, the unborn, morsels of life, cry out:
Do not neglect our presence among you!

By a bard of the bard school

Taize

Make silence to listen to your dream,
hear the Quiet Voice speak of love,
then let words, music, deeds tell the vision

of a time when men and women
honour all creation and their Creator.
Make silence to listen to your dream

and know we are a wilful people
who fail in our own best intentions,
then let words, music, deeds tell the vision.

As we join hands in fellowship
and know again the peace of friendship
make silence to listen to your dream

and the noisy world of hate and conflict
will find a caring serenity
as words, music, deeds tell the vision.

So look at God as Jesus showed us
and learn his way to live for others.
Make silence to listen to your dream,
let words, music, deeds tell the vision.

Kaye Lee

God's Love is Good

And my love said to me, calling me across the moors

Come! Come away with me!

Calling me!

Come out of darkness and through the light winds

We will dust and fly

My light will shine on your face

I long for you, I long to immerse you in my love, in my light

Take my hand and I will capture your heart.

Capture my hand Lord, capture my heart,

Let us be one.

Anna Verey

Trinity

Three persons but one God:
Father, Son and Spirit;
trinity, unity,
great beyond our knowing.

God the Father made us
body, soul, heart and mind,
we are his, his alone
so worship, adore him.

God the Son came to us:
baby, child, perfect man;
cruelly killed, yet alive,
gave us back life with God.

God the Spirit prompts us,
points the path home to God,
takes our hands, places them
on others needing guides.

One true God, three in one,
God, Son, Holy Spirit,
always here, always there,
our past, present, future.

Kaye Lee

III: MOTHER OF THE REDEEMER

What the Kings sought in their wisdom

Of seeking to express

The inexpressible
The Face that writes the heat
Of all Love and the
Sight which wipes
The lines from all limbs and lives;
In one place is put
All Happiness that ever was
And is remembered and longed for
In it's height and depth
Such Space as littles eternity
And contains all possibility
Of blessing that Omnipotence
Could bestow.

All time stands still
Here and is present in a glance
In places seen that have
Not been bound to forgetfulness
By the mercy that is in
His gentlest loving smile.
Here all fathers find
Their title,
Every name is known that
He chooses to gift
And find their truth revealed
No other need remembered
No hunger or thirst save
For closer communion
And to kiss with the
Lips of wonder and worship
And a fire that is love that we eat
And drink most drunk with heavy joy.

These words betray
My ignorance and guesses
And as straw in the flame
Of the Truth:

They burn a little and seem bright
But a while for their
Heat is but pale
To the furnace of Light
They bring back but an echo
But we are not yet real
Or true
And can do but little
With all our gaze
Though it see all the stars of the Heavens
In a single sigh.

Jesus: the Shepherd's Lamb and the Kings' pilgrimage;
His mother's Child; the Is that is God in the eyes of a Babe and Looking out
onto Creation with the Mind of it's Maker, seeking
His friend.

Justin Harmer

The Mystic Rose

From the shanty-towns of India to
The barrios of Havana, the Mystic Rose
Walks in all the glory of her image
Of the God who made her in his own,
And there also walks the man from whom
She came, and from whom later he would come.
The Mystic Rose is grace, the thorns truth.

Andrew Thornton-Norris

Hey Mary!

Bubbling over with God...
So happy...
Like the child you're bringing
Into this world!
That's right - a son!!

You belong to Him alone.
It's the most precious thing,
And
Because of that -
Listen -
To everyone who seeks
A mother's touch
When the tears flow
And when even love hurts
Like a nail going into a young girl's heart.

Justin Harmer

A sword will also pierce your soul

Thunder-candle bearer
You trudge through walls of snow
Perhaps in floaty gauze astonishing children
Perhaps, strong suffering in the worn garmed hood of leper
The flame you bear wards off the roused and ravenous fangs of wolves
Or speaks of warmth and hearth to newly-tamed dogs meek as in the manger
Are these still pagans that mumble their prayers trembling at their wood hut panes– ward off the storm!
That racks our crops, that pillages our hearts and souls –
Sweet Lady, Fierce Benefactress
And what have snow and wolves to do with the Jerusalem you left behind,
But you traverse continents from Simeon's temple, bearing his pronouncement
And you teach all us dark villagers gently
The candle you bear – your child
He will still snow storms on Silesian fields
Spark Northern souls, transform their quality of darkness
Withstand the hoary wind that howls like wolves outside the cabin door
And all the while your wound, the wound of bearing
The dead adult body of a man – shorn from his cross
This knowledge travels with you strengthening, strengthening
As you hold out your beautiful calloused hands
My Mother.

Karolina Stolarska

The song of the Mother Rose, as I thought I heard it whispered.

What song did the Rose sweetly sing
To the flower, o the flower of her Womb -
Did she sing of a thick temple curtain
Flung as wide as the stone of the tomb?

Did the Rose sing an Angel's bright greeting
And the pain of a sword to the heart-
Did she sing of her child lying bleeding
In the arms of a cross and it's art?

Did she sing of the children of slaughter
And the rage of a wild jealous king-
Did she sing of the Father's good daughter
Bearing His Son without sin?

The whisper of God's dearest mother
To her child as she cradled Him close
Was 'I love you as Love loves a lover'
As it was when His eyes came to close.

Justin Harmer

Blessed Among Women

Madonna of the East – you are a bear with her brood
Furious mother – you illuminate the sky above the wretched
Or a modern icon whose stare reflects blood and
Arms upraised - pillars for peace
You are the Black Lady whose dark cheek bears wounds
Dripping with an aureole of bequeathed jewels
Seat of Wisdom – a strong and golden ark

Only the wind on the drying flowers in your chapels
Recalls the sapling girl with a blinding light in a denuded chamber
Her home-spun robe rubbing the earthen floor
As her knees dig deeper into dust
Near shattered by the secret of God's betrothal to the human race
I see you floating on His breeze – a petal
As you say,
Here I am.

Karolina Stolarska

The Lily Song as I thought she let me hear

The Lily she sang as the summer
She sang of the death of her days
She sang of the season of winter
With a catch and a cry like a haze

She sang of a crib like a manger
Of a donkey and Joseph and son
She sang of them fleeing from danger
As the start of the song had begun

She sang of returning to Israel
And the death of a murderous king
And of years spent in peace as a family
All those days how she sweetly would sing

She sang of the woe of a mother
when she lost but a child in the town
And she found a grown man in the temple
And his father all silent with frowns

She sang of the years of His peace
'Ere the fire of his truth was revealed
She sang of the Nazareth table
And the love that it saw yet concealed

She sobbed as she sang of her husband
As the death of his days drew him near
To the arms of his God and His mother
And the earth and the end of his fear

She smiled at the thought of a wedding
And wine springing forth at her word
Like the water of life that was promised
To all who her son loved and heard

She paused at the thought of a promise
That had prophecied pain like a sword
She paused with the pain of a mother

Who will see the cruel death of her Lord

Then her voice in it's prayer sounded fully
With miracles, healings divine
With the water of weak human frailty
Tasting of marvellous wine

She sang of three years spent in joy
As the truth of her song was unveiled
And the cry of her heart sobbed with beauty
Like a ship that does swing as she's sailed

She sang, how she sang of His teaching
The words never bettered or known
Till He held up a glass to man's nature
And showed how with God it is sown:

    The prodigal child of a father
    That longs to return through its shame
    To a love that is wider and larger
    Than any true feeling of blame

The house that is built on His teaching
On the rock of His words and His life
Will survive all the storms and the rivers
That rise as they rise in our strife

But better than this was His love
And His Face and His Heart best of all
And His touch and His Voice like a Dove
That does beckon a mate by it's call

Was it three years she sang like an angel?
And angels were too in her song
But the Lily she sang now of envy
And danger and violence and wrong

For the catch of her song held a note
In her voice like the cry on a Hill
That is heard by the dead as they pass
To the valley of death and are still

And that sound has all manner of terror
Of pain and of sin in its verse
And it sounds for three hours in its horror
A 'music' of sin at its worst

Then the sound of her voice spoke in silence
Three days without hope only sorrow

Then thrilled as she cried like a dawn
That has broken and come a good 'morrow

As dawn; as the sun; as the joy of the spring;
As the sound of a Lover who loves as He sings
At the yellow bright morn which redemption does bring;
How the Mother of God soars with Heavenly Wings;
How the joy of the Heavens is heard in a voice
That is human yet sinless; how her heart does rejoice;

How her song has endured till she paid the full price
All for God, all for Jesus, her Son the sweet Christ.

Justin Harmer

For Feta, who showed me the village on the Croatian island of Vis

'Our Lady of the Pirates', in Komiza

I saw the Oleander and the Tamarisk tree beside the shore.

You took me there at night,
where the shutters of the old stone houses
Creaked with age beneath the yellowing moon.

Our Lady of the Pirates – what a tale you told of the old church
At the far point of the bay
As we came to the stone well.

The pirates, many years ago,
had stolen a painting of the Mother of God

Their ship had sunk
And all that was drawn up from the wrecked boat
Was this image

When the fishermen carried it here and placed it on the ground
A spring burst forth
And here the well was built and now the church.

The image in the candle-lit interior
Is enhanced by many prayers in polyphonic voices
Richly sung by fisherman and women dressed in black.

I wonder that the pirates had the nerve.
How little must they then have known
Of how the universe was woven

As another fisherman's poet wisely said

"Of a thread too bright for the eye".

Take now into your hands this simple cloth
Your life, the one you weave
Of hempen homespun or of gold

And as we sit and spin our tale
Feel tenderly the texture of this cloth
Beneath your hand

And seek within its warp and weft
The thread too bright for the eye,
Divinely planned

For as the last door opens and you leave this world of time
This cloth will be the robe you wear
As the last bell chimes.

Sarah de Nordwall

The song of the Queen and the King's whisper as I thought they did echo to Earth

The Song of the Queen of the Heavens
Is a Song of the Face that's a Heart
That has loved us into life
And love endless and ever new
And full of the joy of a child
That adores and is safe
And yet enventured
Beyond the mere dreams
of Earth

Adventured to a happiness
That swells and mounts and cries
In it's sweetness
Holding all time as it's toy
And the playmates very stars
And all kind
And a feast ever beginning.

Oh the song of the Flower of Heaven
Is a music to shame
all but the stillest small voice...

The whisper of God to His Mother
The child at His side near His Throne...
'I love you as Love loves a lover'
And thus she does know
as she's known.

Justin Harmer

THE ANGELUS

She listened to her angel.
With childlike openness and trust,
Mary heard God's call to bear His Son,
and thus became the mother of us all.

At midday I hear her call:
'Come!
Step outside the burden of yourself
dear wounded child and sit with me'.
Obediently I rest, breathe, and let
her healing love and wisdom
remind me of the promises of God.
Then, with burdens lifted,
I return, at peace, into the world.

At six o'clock when work is done,
her call rings out again.
Our pain and loss is understood,
for Mary suffered all that any mother
could be asked to bear.
Powerless, she stayed beside her son
and watched him crucified -
a laughing stock, an entertainment.

Hour by hour she waited
for his suffering to end.
She waited while they lowered
the dead fruit of her womb
down from the wood.
She held the limp body close to her breast,
before they laid him in a tomb.

Then came the dark nights,
darker day, dense with grief –
hampered by the weight of doubt:
had the sacrifice been in vain?
No. For Mary saw the empty tomb,
then met her son – alive!

And as I learn to listen to my angel,
I can meet Him too.

Helen de Borchgrave

IV: THE PLACE WITHIN

Into the Great Silence

Novices approach
Ask
Are accepted
Into the great silence

Clothed by the tailor
Fed by the cook
Scalped by the barber
Read to by the scholar
Lead by the musician
Shod by the shoemaker
Guided by the fellow journey man

Into the Great Silence
Which leads to Eternity

Jacqui Houlihan

Authentic statement (for Christian bards)

One cannot flee the worldly winds
Two cannot gauge their strength
Three cannot reinvent them
Catch or tame them
Only resist them inwardly

If you want to be authentic
original and eccentric
You'll not find the method marked
my little wandering star

The world's a trap - it owns your
dream before it can be expressed
It laughs at your trials, and
to care and rejoice it affects

No compromise, or clothing
sign, flag, or dance, or even
avoidance of any such things
Alone can break the cardboard box

Under the star nothing new
can be found
It hides openly, until its Creator
be allowed to run free

Reach out then to God
with humility and trusting
And there in your heart, yearning for
Love, will you find Him

Feeding you with His wisdom
the Spirit secreting
Your efforts with
splendour shining and gracing,

The feeling of texture of
newness and flavour
radically simple and

care-less and wonderful
You'll discover:

The calm power to write
paint and consider for free
bestowed by Him who Was
Is
and ever shall be

Piotr Stolarski

'The more sand that has escaped from the hourglass of our life, the clearer we should see through it' [Karol Wojtyła]

and the grains contain the fragments of all i was
and the grains enfold the vision of what i will become

only now is the slipping through the tiny space
only now is the heady rush of the cascading descent

soon to come the fullness of the end
soon to come the containment of the whole

then no more escape
then no more the falling falling sand

in the finishing only clarity
in the finishing only sight

Sarah Fordham

The Icon of Perfection

The Virgin of Gloucester spoke to me and said:

You sin because you love your loneliness.
So love yourself the way three persons love
You and themselves: mind, body and spirit.

Your purity is your happiness,
In contemplation of the eternal,
Live in this and you will never die.

The gift of love is communion
Between all persons earthly and divine,
So go, and give yourself, and be at peace.

Andrew Thornton-Norris

Swimming in the falling star cave

You can only reach the cave by boat.

I was excited by that.

And once you enter in
You leave the brilliant sun outside
And so, the water, although crystal pure
Is dark,
But all the same, I longed to dive right in.

Just then, I looked up
To a tiny opening in the roof of the cave
Where a ray of light pierced through
And shot like a heavenly visitor
Into the water, with miraculous effect.

The light fell like a falling star
And for some reason no one could explain
Deep in the water, formed a bright green star
That sparkled 15 feet beneath the waves.

I dived into the sea
And swam through cool dark water till I saw the green star
With her luminous blue tail
And suddenly brilliant light was on my hands.

I, moving through my darkened underwater cosmos
Struck upon this vein of brilliance

Utterly transfigured, all my being flowed with light.
I, joyous, rose up through the water in the star's bright tail
Till bursting through the surface into air
I felt the light fall radiant on my laughing face.

And treading water in this unexpected glory
Laughed again and reached up into light transfiguring
And cried out to the captain of the boat
"Is this how we arrive in heaven,
Emerging from the watery dark whilst following the star
Unique to us?"

The surface of the water, crossed by light,
Refracted on the cave's roof,
Danced with accompanying delight

And I, returning to my boat once more
Moved off into the dark baptismal water of the cave

And from the benediction of the falling star
Found all the sparkling sea, cold on my flesh,
Preparing me for resurrected life,
And tingling with the brightening salt of grace.

Sarah de Nordwall

Wisdom and the Museums (or Free Thought)

Squareset columns, to drive all that who what when
Into the Future, which shall be Art Deco
(What other reason to spend all that money on
A Museum of Art of the City?).
They crumble now
Dusting the boards over the windows,
And even the keep-out barriers
Are tottering in the breeze,
Making no more noise than the
Discarded newspaper which shouted
Choose a dictator
Choose a dictator
Choose a dictator
And they did as they were told
And they chose a dictator
And they chose Pétain
And they got the one they chose
And then *Sorry, your dictator is temporarily unavailable:*
Please hold while we try to connect you.

Stop look listen
The Impasse of Billy is open for you
Cross to the new museum on the Quai Branly.

And we did as we were told
And we crossed and saw through a glass
And we entered, and behold
A jungle, and we smiled at an artist's whimsy:
A fibreglass giraffe grinning over greenery.
And look, a seat
And listen, music, music to make you dance and see the leaves
But then the two moustaches came solid out from the trees
(This Latin American jungle is so authentic)
Please go down and sit, a concert is going on.
No movement, only a presence just inside my space
And reinforcements only an earpiece away
So we went down (only one way, the others are fenced off).

And we sat for our magical mystical tour of music of the world
And we could clap and swing in time
And after the half-hour choose
To go inside for a world arranged
Or drink exotic cordials
Bottled in Hayes (Middlesex).

And I sought after Wisdom
And I found her not.
Sorry, there is a fault.
Please try later.

Fr Dominic White, OP

bounded by what is beyond me and bitten by what is within

bounded by what is beyond me and bitten by what is within
i left the house quietly
the hush of evening spread before me like a carpet of many graces

Sarah Fordham

Soul-tree

I have a strong desire
To learn the ways
Of the ego-less warrior
Who dreams and
Acknowledges the Truth
To make me wise
And embody principles
To nourish me
Along my journey.

Despite my fears
I promise to be
An artist who
Believes in Paradise
And the fulfillment
Of God's vision
For the Beloved
To move our hearts
To feel His love.

Our life is held
In the balance
Of wit and whim
Whilst our memories
Play on the loom
Of our minds
Sometimes free
Sometimes close
Like a tiny doll.

I listen to the song
Of the cherry tree
As it serenades
The silent Cause
Of our revolving
Spirits, and breathe
As the daffodils open
Among the Wakener
Who rustles the world.

Tom Bentall

The Communion of Saints

The element in which the spirit lives,
Like fish in water, birds in air, is this:
Silence, where communion is not
With those on earth, but is in solitude.

The element in which happiness
Exists is contemplation, where we see
The nature of the universe within
Reflected in the universe without.

Andrew Thornton-Norris

Eggonizing

At dawn
I touch the hard shell of today...

Will I warm it gently in my hands
Until I feel the pulse of inner space
Hatching a heart for all that is?

Will I expose the contents bare
And paint the confines of my emptiness
With the healing shades of the Easter Mysteries?

Or will I squeeze it hard with greed
Breaking the promise that you keep
Despite the fragmented nature of my engagement?

At night
I lay waste under the stars...

The yoke of today nourished my dreams
Linking my heart with the yellow brick road
Fading in virgin milky Way

Monika Chmelova

Diapause

Like an elegant tomb in lustrous blue
It hangs suspended bauble-bullet
Drawing the eye into its smooth immutability &
Endless mourning
An inner twilight whose scenes can only be imagined.

Birth

Brash sunrise of commonality
Gharish every day
Lava hued wings with white spots
Like blights
Oblivious of its ugliness it
Straddles blank-faced garden flowers
An awkward jarring song of the soul –
A plebeian psalm
It beats it futile wings
And movement becomes
Illumination

Karolina Stolarska

Empty tomb- *before the empty tabernacle of Good Friday*

There's no life.
What once was life is no more.
Tomb broken, death is done.
All that is left is silence, void- empty tomb.
Life was taken, robbed, unknown
No meaning explains this barren scene.
Bring back the body,
let me grieve a while longer!
Do not take that which for me is certain!
Life is gone, but so is death now.
Do not look among death for what is no longer dead.
My void is real Lord.
What was once life, had died, gone, taken.
Only deafening silence and void remains.
an aching hole where my past life has been.
Grieve it, but don't stay.
What has been taken cannot be replaced.
But hope cannot be taken.
What is void and death and silence,
nothing,
is only the beginning.
I am your God and will make
something from nothing.
This is the place where the story starts not ends.
Some things can never die-
do not believe it any other way.

Kate Golding

Small places (after St Therese of Lisieux)

I have travelled on silver threads
along steel furnishings
and carpet islands
which hold tinkling keys
and bell-tones under the boards.
The grouting peeled away
my feet touched stone.
A voice meant company
so I scurried up the skirting
and later, playing with marble spinners
my cat looked on
as the visitor and his news
spelt mischief in my life

Now, when I remember those times
I have only the silence
of small places

Tom Bentall

Noonday Shiver

I will not be afraid of the terror by night,
Or the arrow that flies by day,
Or the pestilence that stalks in darkness,
Or the destruction that lays waste at noon ...

When it comes
The windless shiver
I send it away
And am warmed by your wood
Burning:
Fire in the desert
Presence in my heart

Sarah Fordham

The Chair

I recognised my mother's chair:
stained and worn
it belonged to my old life
when I lived, inadequately,
in anxious fear – unforgiven.

In Italy , that summer,
on the feast of Santa Clara ,
I clearly saw my mother
sitting in this chair –
enlightened.

As the mass continued -
celebrating the girl
who gave up wealth and privilege
to live in holy poverty like
her soul-mate Francis of Assisi -
I looked, and looked,
until I realised that my mother -
who needed wealth and privilege -
was being embraced
by light and life and love.

Three days later, in England ,
my mother died.

Re clothed in gold
the chair is mine now.
Here I sit, and breathe,
while silence heals -
till we can both reflect
the radiance of eternity.

Helen de Borchgrave

Logics

You don't make sense
and you don't fit,
neither in my logic's grid,
nor in my learnt vocabulary.

But you are Sense and without you,
I've not much left to say:
words become masks
that cover an empty silence.

Come break the grill
and like a parent or a lover
teach me new meanings
to open my mind's window to your breeze.

Catherine Cruz, FMVD

Wisdom and the Museums: an unexpected postscript

Modern art has as many rules as the city:
Once the work is done, you mustn't go back to the source of inspiration
It will be inherently disappointing,
A void too empty even to make a Rothko:
For it is not the same as itself.
(Sorry, can't help you there, the philosophers are as unavailable
As the dictator himself.)
And do not gaze on the object
Because now it has done its work
You are in the phase of memory
Which works you.

Well, at least there are some causes
Which have no need of earpieces for reinforcement.
But Wisdom is always playing around the creation
So that Sunday afternoon I broke the rules, the lot.
Back to the Museum of the City:
There were the hoodies, leaping their skateboards
Over the sky-puddles in the broken paving.
(I said to myself, has Paris become the new Peckham?)

And for all the boardings-up and the barriers, there was one window
And there I saw people. As the hoodies danced around me
Like the angels for Rabbi Eleazar,
I found the door. Inside were crowds,
It was free, the officer at the electronic arch did nothing
As all the people were secure enough.

Walls of Matisses, and some mad stuff too,
But around the Throne they take all that in their stride,
And I rejoiced
That Wisdom has built her house
And that I have a right to be wrong.

Fr Dominic White, OP

Lenten Longing

I ache for my dear ones' happiness
and mine
But deeper than that, I ache for God
with a bruised heart

I ache for the Love that can embrace without reserve
to touch
and be touched
even when there is no life at fingertips

I ache for the wholeness that does not come
from remaining unbroken
although it exposes fears of waste
So I ache for that God who gathers the crumbs of my life
into a mystery worth dying for

I also ache for an acute connection
with the Life that grows in me
and around me
I long to nurture it and be nurtured by it

I ache for the confidence
to trust the current I cannot see
and learn to swim with it

I ache for the space to taste the peace
deeper than the earth's core
even from the vintage point of my spinning days

I ache for the wisdom to know
when my step out of sync
means faithfulness
and when it marks out betrayal

I ache for a profound transformation
that would open new ways
of expressing my gratitude

Monika Chmelova

Ordinary Epiphany

Lifting up the four corners of my room
It mounts the urban sky
A sea of clouds within, without
I can feel the world turning
Lapped with molten waves of setting Sun
I can hear countless heartbeats
Pink embers pale on the wide lunar landscape of my bed
I'm left a water-lily floating in Otherness
Higher than the aeroplane overhead
Its drone drowned
by the splash of glass dissolving

Karolina Stolarska

Part Three of Strange In Deed:
The Garden Tomb

The tomb was empty of all but light

And the sunshine blessed the opening in the roof of the tomb
Like a messenger from a brighter world.

And in the absence of everyone else
Both the living and the dead

Whose endless needs and questions had been oppressing me darkly
With the weight of their centuries of unresolvable agonies

They were suddenly present.

They were there

They has blossomed instantaneously into being
Unquestionably

As simple as sunflowers

The Five Words

For the feeding of seven times seventy thousand
And power was in them
And I knew it then

"Love is stronger than death"

Let's hear it again!

Love Is Stronger Than Death

Amen
            Amen
                        Amen.

Sarah de Nordwall

Touching the Lord

For Karol Wojtyła

:and so it comes, the end
:deeply embedded in the beginning
:a line within the mind
:a deep fissure in the heart
:the knowledge of it flickering
:the flame extending
:as the candle slowly burns
:and the shadows lengthen
:and so it comes, the end

:life, a shallow sea to swim in
:before the disappearance into the deep

Sarah Fordham

Postscript:
What is the connection between the Bard School and this anthology?

Many of the people contributing to this anthology have been touched by elements of the training and community offered through the Bard School over the last 5 years. Some may have been taking part in conversations on the Bard School Google-list with other Christian artists, to inspire them in their journey to become professional artists, rooted in grace.

The idea of the Bard School was given to me when I was a primary school teacher many years ago. Dusting the library shelves, I came across a book called *The Way of the Story Teller* by Ruth Sawyer. It explained about the 8th-century bards in Ireland who stood at the heart of their spiritual and political communities using poetry, story and song to inspire and challenge, entertain and provoke. What a fantastic job, I thought. When do I start?

But what would a Christian Bard be like and how could one train to become one? There were prophets in Ancient Israel, such as Nathan, who told stories to reach the king's conscience. Ezekiel even used many forms of what today would be called 'performance and installation art' to make his point. Musicians were summoned to use their music for healing and even for the discernment of political strategy. And David danced for Ha Shem before the Ark.

The ancient Irish bards had bard schools which prepared them to be both academically learned as well as spontaneous, spiritual and political, comedic and serious. They were even encouraged to attain 'the virtues of all classes and the vices of none'! But where could one go to train today in such an enlightened way - that consciously developed the spiritual gifts within the artistic life?

Well, it took me many years to fathom out a few responses to these questions and to learn from many others en route who were trying similar projects; from 'King David Kompany' in Croydon, to 'Intermission' in Knightsbridge, from the teachings on Rhapsodic Theatre by John Paul II, to experiments in alternative cabaret with 'Moot'. But in 2006 the Bard School began at Corpus Christi church on the feast day of Our Lady of Lourdes with Tom Bentall, Anna Johnstone and myself under the kind ministrations of Fr Antonio Ritaccio, who said Mass and made the soup. We brought together a few key elements - time for friendship and food, time for Mass and the silent prayer of Adoration, and then through workshops and artistic session we engaged, over the months, with five equally important lines of enquiry, most of which we felt we had missed out on during our respective artistic trainings –

1) Theology and Philosophy – why they matter to art and the human person.
2) The mystery of the artistic process – what does it reveal about us and about God?
3) The nature of the artistic vocation and its calling to society.
4) Our own journey of personal healing – what is it and how does it happen? How does our personal maturity affect our capacities as artists?
5) The arts business, its ethics and its possibilities. What kind of an artist/creative do I want to be and what is the abundant life? Does money matter?

Some of the contributors to this anthology have taken part in sessions created to explore all of these strands. It's an ongoing process and resources and expertise are building up, but we are always looking for more contributors, who can help with the teaching and the questioning. But at the heart of it all, I think most of us have found that, as we all move at different paces and come from different places, that the most important gift is finding an environment where you can be unafraid to state that the needs of your heart are truly important. This is why friendship is at the heart of the Bard School. This is why I loved the icon that Martin Earle included in a dissertation that he was writing. Details of it are featured as elements of the cover designed by his brother Leo Earle. People; men, women and angels are engaged in profound and happy conversation – authentic and joyful. This is Giovanni di Paolo's vision of Paradise.

It is more difficult, it seems, but also I think more important, to learn to love, than it is to be a virtuoso or a great artistic success. True teaching and learning, performing and doing business, I believe can be fostered best in an environment of love. It is not a foolish dream to hope and work for such a blessed reality. Victor Frankl, psychiatrist and Holocaust survivor makes this comment in his book *Man's Search for Meaning*:

> *No one can become fully aware of the very essence of another human being unless he loves him. By the spiritual act of love he is enabled to see the essential traits and features in the beloved person: and even more, he sees that which is potential in him, that which is not yet actualized but yet ought to be actualised. Furthermore, by his love, the loving person enables the beloved*

person to actualize these potentialities.

To love in the midst of hatred is a great victory. To love in the midst of indifference and confusion is also rather a trial. But loving oneself is also a task in itself: the one most often avoided. The consequences of this evasion can be seen in burnout, loneliness, a sense of futility in the midst of activity and a sense of never being enough. These things can be mitigated however, both by an honest and authentic community and a revealing artistic process, that slips under the ego's guard and speaks truth to the heart.

Jesus told stories. His metaphors sprung from the very depths of his engagement with ordinary life and His intimacy with the life of the Father. The strength of this relationship gave Him the courage and compassion to speak what needed to be spoken, whether to Governors, High Priests, ordinary folk or to local prostitutes. His prayer life informed His artistry and both came from the heart, whilst being profoundly intelligent.

I was thrilled when Piotr said he wanted to pull together a collection of poems from bards and friends of bards, to mark the beatification of John Paul II. John Paul II's vision of the artist as one who can share unique theological insights and who is called to 'awaken the enthusiasm and energies necessary to meet and master the challenges of the age' has been a key inspiration in my life and that of many other artists. When I met John Paul II in Rome in a small gathering in the 1980s, he put aside his prepared speech and took up a sheet of the lyrics of the songs we had been singing for him. He found a line in Italian that he kept repeating and he said 'Look at these words – *dentro di noi* – from within us – from within us!' He was calling us to pay attention and to value that which lay within us, for we were created in the image of God and our gifts, awoken by the Spirit are a very important piece in the puzzle that is the hope of mankind – the Body of Christ. Is this to take ourselves and our work too seriously? The Holy Father didn't think so. He called all of us even higher than this, to the beauty of an aspiration to know the Holiness of God as profoundly, passionately and joyfully as the Saints themselves.

He then reminded us that our passions and talents were not only God's gift to us, but that we had a journey to make before these talents could truly become gifts for others.

So we hope that there have been poems or even just lines in this anthology that have touched your heart in some way or inspired you to write something even better and send it to the Bard School, or even better, to come along and show us how it's done! It's the conversation that is started by any work of art that is one of the things I look forward to. So thanks for joining in and staying with us this far. See you on the blogs for news of your creations and our on-going explorations.

Sarah de Nordwall - A bard with a bard school

sdenordwall@yahoo.co.uk

http://sarahdenordwall.blogspot.com

http://thebardschool.blogspot.com

CONTRIBUTORS

Tom BENTALL trained in Jazz piano at Leeds College of Music and Guildhall. He has taken up poetry more seriously since joining the Bard School, becoming a Catholic and attending the Poetry School. He values his Persian heritage and is also passionate about music therapy.

Monika CHMELOVA is originally from Slovakia. She has been a lay member of the Verbum Dei Community since 2001, and currently works for the Catholic Church as an Advisor for Catechesis & Adult Formation. She paints images with words and colours in a variety of settings, inspired by both Life and the Scripture.

Catherine CRUZ, FMVD grew up in London and Portsmouth. After graduating from Durham University, she became a Catholic and not long afterwards joined the Verbum Dei Community. She has worked pastorally in Spain, USA and England and is presently based with her community in Southampton where she is a University Chaplain.

Bess TWISTON DAVIES is a freelance journalist who edits the online Faith page of The Times newspaper, and *t!* an alternative magazine for teenage girls. A member of the Christian arts group, the Bard School, she is also writing a lighthearted novella, set in a tropical Republic near Birmingham.

Helen DE BORCHGRAVE studied Fine Art Conservation and worked as a private conservator. She is a member of A.I.C.A. (International Art Critics), and has written for various publications including Country Life, Catholic Herald and the Jewish Chronicle. For 15 years she led Art Tours in Europe, and published *A Journey into Christian Art* (1999).

Sarah DE NORDWALL is a Bard with a Bard school http://thebardschool.blogspot.com. She creates poems and stories for live performance in political and personal settings. Her *CD Lipstick is a Spiritual Experience* is available on her blog http://sarahdenordwall.blogspot.com and she is currently recording two new CDs and forming a Rhapsodic Theatre company.

Martin EARLE studied animation at the Royal College of Art and now lives in a L'Arche community in France, as an assistant to adults with learning difficulties.

Jonathan FORDHAM is a Brighton-based poet who graduated from the University of Kent at Canterbury with an MA in Modern Literature. Having worked in book publishing, he now works in education as an inclusion mentor. He is particularly interested in the convergence of monasticism and social action.

Sarah FORDHAM is a workshop facilitator and seminar speaker, regularly preaching and teaching on biblical subjects at home and abroad. Sarah has published *Psalm Readings (2005), The Cool of the Day (2009)* and *Love's First Look (*2010). She co-chairs the Churches Spirituality Co-ordinating Group and is part of the writers' group for the Week of Christian Unity. Her Masters dissertation is on the poetry of Karol Wojtyła.

Kate GOLDING spent 8 years working with a Catholic community called Verbum Dei in Europe and the US and some time studying Philosophy at Blackfriars, Oxford. Since leaving the community she now works with autistic children and plans to pursue a career in education.

Justin HARMER enjoys a portfolio career in the arts. He sings Bass in a range of styles from Opera to pop and folk, teaches piano, plays guitar and organ and composes. Since being received into the Catholic Church in 2009, he has written much poetry; some published, some performed and some exhibited.

Michael HOARE lives in Essex. After serving in the army he worked in various jobs, including the building trade. He joined the Sion Catholic Community for Evangelisation with his wife, where they were core members for 10 years. Writing poetry for many years, he now mainly writes what he calls Prayer Poems.

Jacqui HOULIHAN is an active member of St Thomas of Canterbury church, Fulham. A member of the choir, she helps with RCIA (Rite of Christian Initiation for Adults). She sews and embroiders rosary pockets, knits, and participates in the Charismatic Renewal.

Jean HUBERT is a 44 year-old Frenchman who loves meeting people, exploring and writing. God changed his life into a pilgrim's adventure and gave him new dispositions for social issues and creativity (thanks to Sr Sheila's art classes too).

Paula JORDAO, FMVD has been a Verbum Dei missionary since 1990. Her deepest desire is that every person might experience God's personal love. That's why she prays, preaches, sings and tries to give her whole life to God and his people. She's been in England for 10 years now, with some breaks in other countries.

Kaye LEE is an Australian and a retired nurse who lives in North London. She has had poems published in various magazines and anthologies. She also writes hymns, some of which have been used in services at Methodist Central Hall, Westminster where she is an active member.

Gabriel OLEARNIK is of Polish descent and was raised in England and educated in London. His background includes medieval literature, history, the law and time in both Warsaw and Kraków. His work has previously appeared in *Dappled Things* (Pushcart Prize nominee). His first book of poetry, *Amor de Lohn*, received critical acclaim. *Gunpowder Square*, his second book, is forthcoming.

Karolina STOLARSKA combines a background in philosophy and theology, making art and poetry and facilitating experiential workshops. Inspired by John Paul II's works and the Bard School she is interested in bringing together revealed truth and the personal and existential. She is currently training in art therapy. www.karolinastolarska.blogspot.com

Piotr STOLARSKI, founder of *Tignarius Publications*, is a Catholic historian and poet. He completed a PhD (2008), published *Friars on the Frontier* – a study of the Dominicans in the Polish Counter-Reformation (Ashgate, 2010), and the poetry collection *Twilight of the Idols* (2011). He works in public libraries, and occasionally as a volunteer.

Andrew THORNTON-NORRIS is the author of *The Spiritual History of English*, in which he argues that today's social and cultural decay is the result of the death of Protestantism in the 1960's. He is also the author of a collection of poems, *The Walled Garden*, and *The Ghost of Identity*, a novel.

Anna VEREY is 27 years old. She currently lives in London, in the sunny borough of East Dulwich, home of the babyccino. Her mother is from Vienna and her father is from Berkshire and her sense of identity feels multi-national and busy like the M25.

Dominic WHITE's poems are from two of his collections: *Journeys Across Reality*, about what happens when you travel, and *The Wisdom Poems*, on what happens when you stop. He is also a composer and choreographer, and founder-director of the Cosmos dance project www.cosmosdance.com. He is a Catholic priest and Dominican friar.

ACKNOWLEDGMENTS

All poems and supplementary material Copyright © Contributors 2012, unless otherwise dated or previously published:

'Choose Freedom' Copyright © Helen de Borchgrave, 2009

'Which World?' Copyright © Helen de Borchgrave, 2009

'The Angelus' Copyright © Helen de Borchgrave, 2008

'The Chair' Copyright © Helen de Borchgrave, 2008

'The Wasted Tree' Copyright © Sarah de Nordwall, 2008

'Push aside the Terror of Things to be Done' Copyright © Sarah de Nordwall, 2009

''Our Lady of the Pirates', in Komiza' Copyright © Sarah de Nordwall, 2006

'Swimming in the falling star cave' Copyright © Sarah de Nordwall, 2006

'Part Three of Strange In Deed: The Garden Tomb' Copyright © Sarah de Nordwall, 1999

'Touching the Lord' Copyright © Sarah Fordham, 2005

'Wisdom of the wayside….' Copyright © Kate Golding, 2006

'Tender God' Copyright © Kate Golding, 2006

'Empty Tomb' Copyright © Kate Golding, 2007

'Into the Great Silence' Copyright © Jacqui Houlihan, 2007

'[The] Priest-Machine' and 'Byzantium' from *Amor De Lonh* (Andromache Books, 2009) Copyright © Gabriel Olearnik, 2009

Editor’s Note

This anthology was put together in three months (February-April 2011) – something made possible by email and the internet. I would like to thank all the contributors for their generosity and cooperation. For their attendance and input at the coordination meeting, thanks to Monika Chmelova, Bess Twiston Davies, Sarah de Nordwall, Sarah Fordham, Justin Harmer, and Karolina Stolarska. I am grateful to Fr Dominic for improving the introduction, and would like to thank Sarah Fordham for discussing the layout and sharing information about publishing. As an associate of the Bard School myself, I am also grateful to Sarah de Nordwall for flying the banner for Christian arts and culture and inspiring many of the contributors with her vision. Finally, special thanks to Leo Earle and Claire Barrie for their cover design and typographical work for the first edition. (This second edition features a different typography.) A.M.D.G. ✠ 2012 A.D.

Te decet hymnus Deus in Sion
Et tibi reddetur votum in Jerusalem!

www.ingramcontent.com/pod-product-compliance
Ingram Content Group UK Ltd.
Pitfield, Milton Keynes, MK11 3LW, UK
UKHW020127250726
13967UKWH00002B/521

9 781471 621314